T0131971

How to Get to Heaven in Three Easy Steps...
...Really!

DIANE A. MUMFORD

WestBow Press books may be ordered through booksellers or by contacting:

WestBow Press
A Division of Thomas Nelson & Zondervan
1663 Liberty Drive
Bloomington, IN 47403
www.westbowpress.com
1 (866) 928-1240

Because of the dynamic nature of the Internet, any web addresses or links contained
in this book may have changed since publication and may no longer be valid. The views
expressed in this work are solely those of the author and do not necessarily reflect the
views of the publisher, and the publisher hereby disclaims any responsibility for them.

Any people depicted in stock imagery provided by Getty Images are models,
and such images are being used for illustrative purposes only.
Certain stock imagery © Getty Images.

Scriptures taken from the Holy Bible, New International Version®, NIV®. Copyright © 1973,
1978, 1984, 2011 by Biblica, Inc.™ Used by permission of Zondervan. All rights reserved
worldwide. www.zondervan.com The "NIV" and "New International Version" are trademarks
registered in the United States Patent and Trademark Office by Biblica, Inc.™

ISBN: 978-1-9736-9642-1 (sc)
ISBN: 978-1-9736-9643-8 (e)

Library of Congress Control Number: 2020913205

Print information available on the last page.

WestBow Press rev. date: 09/26/2020

WESTBOW
P R E S S®
A DIVISION OF THOMAS NELSON
& ZONDERVAN

Train your children in the Way they should go and when they are old they will not turn from it.

Proverbs 22:6

A little girl went to her Grandma's funeral.
Her name is Sophie and she is 10 years old!

As Sophie listened to the Pastor speak, she heard him say that he knew her Grandma was in heaven among the angels and sitting with Jesus! "We know this", the Pastor continued, "because she was a woman of faith. Faith is believing in something even though we can't see it."

At that point, Sophie asked her parents, "If you can't see faith, how do you know she really had faith? "That's a good question, Sophie, said Dad. I think you need to ask someone who might have the answer.

After the funeral, Sophie asked several people. "Do you know what faith is? Her friend, Sydney, said, "I think it has something to do with church." Her cousin, Chloe, said, "Maybe it has something to do with angels." She even asked the cashier at the grocery store who said "Maybe you should ask someone who is really old."

Finally, Sophie decided that since the Pastor had talked about faith, he should be the one to ask. So off to church she went.

Sophie knocked on the Pastor's door. "Come on in Sophie, he said, what's on your mind?"

"You said that you knew my Grandma was in heaven because she had something called faith and that faith was believing in what you couldn't see. I don't understand. If you can't see it, how can you believe it??"

"Good question, Sophie! I'm so glad you asked me, said the Pastor, let me tell you how I know. My eyes don't tell me but my heart does."

"How does your heart tell you?" Asked Sophie.

"A long time ago when I was about your age, I asked Jesus to come into my heart and be the Lord and Savior of my life." "Why would you want to do that?" Sophie questioned.

"Well", said the Pastor, "I knew something was missing from my life. I didn't know what it was but my heart felt very empty. So, I asked different people if they knew what faith was. I got lots of answers but none really answered my question. I finally decided to ask my Pastor. He always said he was in the business of helping hearts feel better! So, I figured he was the one to ask."

My Pastor said, "When your heart feels like there is something missing, it's because you haven't asked Jesus to live inside it!"

"REALLY!!, how can He do that??", Sophie's eyes got big as she asked.

"It's very easy," the Pastor said, "let me tell you how. <u>First</u>, you have to ask Jesus to forgive all the things you've done or said that were wrong. You know what they are and so does He. You just have to say you're sorry and that you'll be better and think before you might do or say something you know you shouldn't. <u>Second</u>, you need to ask Jesus to be a part of your life. Not just some parts like your nose or your toes, but every single part. That's when He will come and live in your heart! And <u>Third</u>, you need to say thank you to Jesus for giving you the best gift ever!"

"That's it!! From then on Jesus will live in your heart and be with you forever. You can count on His promises because He said, 'Never will I leave you and never will I let you go, you are mine for eternity'. Do you know where eternity is, Sophie? It's in heaven! Your Grandma asked Jesus to live in her heart many years ago. It was her faith in what she couldn't see here on earth but what she knew she would see in heaven that she always believed. That's why I know your Grandma is in heaven."

Sophie looked at the Pastor and said, "I'm sorry I've done and said some wrong things. I want Jesus to live in my heart forever and I thank Him very much."

And on that very day, Jesus came to live with Sophie right inside her heart......Really!

Sophie's Heart

(hold up to the light)

JESUS

Printed in the United States
By Bookmasters